Celine Dion

LET'S TALK ABOUT LOVE

THIS IS A CARLTON BOOK

Text and design copyright © Carlton Books Limited 1998
This edition published by Carlton Books Limited 1998

A CIP catalogue for this book is available from the British Library

ISBN 1 85868 593 1 Paperback
ISBN 1 85868 581 8 Hardback

Project Editor: Lucian Randall
Copy Editor: Allie Glenny
Senior Art Editor: Zöe Maggs
Design: Simon Balley
Picture Research: Lorna Ainger
Production: Alexia Turner

Printed and bound in Italy

10 9 8 7 6 5 4 3 2 1

Picture Credits

The publishers would like to thank the following sources
for their kind permission to reproduce the pictures in
this book:

All Action Pictures 52/Gareth Davies 44, Simon
Meaker 42, 43, Susan Moore 58, Paul Smith 3, 53

Corbis UK Ltd./David Allen 50, Patsy Lynch 30, Pacha
55, Neelie Sacharow 28, Marko Shark 10

London Features International Ltd./David Fisher 7, 46,
Gregg De Guire 13, 34, Kevin Mazur 60

Pictorial Press Limited/Nancy Kaszerman 64, Jeffrey
Mayer 41, 66

Retna Pictures Limited/Fitzroy Barret 32, Steve Eichner
27, Chris Vooren 16

Rex Features Ltd. 5l, 5c, 9, 19, 22, 25, 35, 36/P.Doyle
67, Gaia 47, 48, Robert Galbraith 39, Ken Mckay 4, 62,
David Niviere 69, Raddatz 31, Brian Rasic 5r, Sipa 57,
Still Press Agency/Serge Arnal 68, Villard/Niviere 45,
Villard 49

S.I.N./Eyecontact 65
Every effort has been made to acknowledge correctly
and contact the source and/or copyright holder of each
picture, and Carlton Books Limited apologises for any
unintentional errors or omissions which will be correct-
ed in future editions of this book.

Celine Dion

LET'S TALK ABOUT LOVE

JEREMY DEAN

CARLTON

Contents

The emotion of simple love songs is an international language, a mode of communication that can transcend the often clumsy and hackneyed sentiment of a pop lyric or convey the depth and intensity of a sincere sonnet. Sometimes, a practitioner of this familiar format finds a voice capable of imbuing these songs with enough magic to strike a chord that resounds in the heartstrings of the masses irrespective of their class, creed, colour, or native tongue. The heart of Celine Dion has been filled with love and music from its first beatings.

Song came from her before she could speak. Though in those early days there was little to mark her out from any other child of a similar background, gradually it became apparent that this ordinary French-Canadian girl had a particular talent, a talent that would one day be recognized by millions of people throughout the world. That talent was the unquantifiable essence which found expression through her voice. Though intangible and unnameable, that essence was to become the precious saleable com-

Introduction

modity that now ensures that the name Celine Dion is on the lips of millions of loyal fans.

There was nothing remarkable about a young French-Canadian singing and enjoying sharing music with her relatives and family friends. Father played accordion, mother played violin, and each of her siblings sang and played instruments. They were all talented and played semi-professionally in local venues. Celine has since commented that she is not the most talented of her family, 'just the luckiest'. Yet despite her famed down-to-earth modesty, Celine Dion displayed a most unusual, and definitely remarkable, talent from her earliest years. She was just five years old when she gave her first public performance.

Throughout Canada there is a long established folk tradition. It would be more unusual for a youngster brought up against such a backdrop *not* to sing or play an instrument. This, of course, makes it all the more remarkable when any individual rises above the rest and, after becoming a local home-grown favourite, goes on to become one of the world's top-selling artists. This is what Celine Dion has done.

Inside the pop-diva-superstar still resides the little girl with her family values and humble beginnings. Interviewers and biographers have dug into her past and talked to her friends and acquaintances looking for some factor as sensational as her success, maybe a blemish of character or dark secret, but to no avail. So what is it about Celine Dion that appeals so widely? The clues lie within her story. A story of love, romance, humanity, compassion, toil, and consuming ambition which has carried Celine Dion from child prodigy to multi-award-winning international recognition, culminating in a performance before a vast television audience exceeding three and a half billion, and earning her the prestigious Order of Canada.

ABOVE: *Celine Dion: inside the pop-diva still resides a little girl with family values.*

eline's charmed life began on 30 March 1968. She was born and raised in Charlemagne, a satellite town 30 km east of Montreal in the Canadian province of Québec. Charlemagne is a small, quiet place with a population of around 6,000. Even her name came from music, taken from the Hugues Auffray song, 'Céline'. With eight sisters and five brothers, the baby of the Dion family was given a warm welcome into the world.

Like most French-speaking Québecois, her parents were Catholic. Her father, Adhemar, had not intended to start a large family when he married Thérèse Tanguay. In fact, he had not really intended to have any children, but his wife obviously had different plans and convinced him otherwise. Or maybe, as Celine once jested, 'You know, there was no television at the time, no radio, so what else?'

Her father had various occupations—meat inspector, lumberjack, security man, semi-professional folk musician—but eventually settled into running the family

I was dreaming

restaurant. All the family would prepare food, wait tables, provide the music, and take turns at singing.

The first time Celine Dion sang for an audience larger than her immediate family was at the wedding of her brother, Michel. She was just five years of age and can remember the feeling she had when, after all the concentration and effort she had put into the song, she was rewarded with an enthusiastic and appreciative round of applause. It was then that she realized this was what she was meant to do. Her destiny was laid out before her.

It was at the family diner, Le Vieux Baril, that Celine began to come to the attention of her public. As a five-year-old, possessing a voice of unusual power for her age, she took to singing her favorite songs there. She used a table-top as her stage and chose

OPPOSITE: *Adhemar and Thérèse Dion, Celine's much-loved parents.*

her songs from those she heard at home. The songs of Québec star Ginette Reno were a popular choice and soon became the young Celine's favourite.

The little girl with the big, belting voice soon became the major attraction at the Dions' restaurant, and by the time she was approaching 12 years of age people would ask when she was likely to perform before booking their tables. It soon became apparent that when Celine sang business boomed, and Celine became famous locally, known as 'la p'tite Québecoise'.

On warm evenings, the show would take place in the back yard and involve all the available members of the Dion family playing their various instruments, often with Celine singing. Sometimes nearby residents would complain of the noise and the police would arrive to check things out. Celine remembers that the officers were friendly, and 'they would always stop and have a drink with us.'

Although the family business flourished, the money it brought in did not go far toward keeping a family of 16, and the Dions knew hardship, having to struggle for a living in those early days. Their music brought in much-needed extra cash through

performances at local functions, parties, and weddings. Adhemar usually played the accordion, while Thérèse played violin, and the children took turns at playing other instruments or singing.

The family found it difficult to visit their friends and relations—there were too many of them to fit into a car, and a family of 16 descending for Sunday lunch could be a bit of an imposition—so instead, most weekends their friends and relatives came to them. This made the family even larger on weekends, and especially for Sunday dinner, when the extended family throng would enjoy Thérèse's legendary hams and specially prepared meats.

The door was always open to family and friends, and there was a good reason for this. The entire family were musicians and performers, and the older children often played at functions or local clubs. This meant that they came home late and at differ-

ABOVE: *In reflective mood: Celine in 1991.*

ent times. Celine remembers that her mother would lie in bed half-awake, hearing and recognizing each set of footsteps until the whole family was accounted for, home, in bed, and safe.

'We were never poor, but we slept three or four kids in the same bed. It was fantastic,' Celine fondly reminisces. 'We had everything we wanted: love, affection, attention, smart parents, and music. I think that when there is music in your life, there's happiness.'

With mother, father, and 13 brothers and sisters playing instruments and singing, Celine must have enjoyed much music and happiness. All her family before her had taken to the stage.

'They all sang before me,' Celine has stated. 'Everybody plays everything. Both parents used to tour with members of the family. It helped to pay the bills at the end of the month, but they were doing it because they loved doing it.'

Celine has only fond memories of her childhood at home: 'There was love, music, the smell of food, affection.' Away from the comforts of this environment, and the love of her parents and siblings she felt diminished.

Meal-times were a particular pleasure of Celine's. Three times every day the entire family sat round the huge kitchen table together to enjoy fine, wholesome food. Nearly always, at some point in the meal, the family would begin to play tunes using knives and forks and their partially-drained glasses. Everyone drank at a different rate, so each glass made a particular note, and if a note was needed that could not be found, then someone would drink a little more until the correct sound was achieved.

The Dion children were raised as Catholics, though were not strict church-goers. They were at church often enough with babies to be christened and weddings to attend, but there was a certain degree of resentment toward the church as an establishment. This may have stemmed from a priest who seemed a little too keen to interfere with the Dions' private family life. Apparently, some while after the first three children had been born to Mr and Mrs Dion, the local priest called to inquire why a fourth child was not yet on the way; months had passed and Thérèse was not yet pregnant again. Quite understandably, Thérèse told the priest that she and her husband would decide when to have their next child and would take into account the good of the family as a whole. Being a Catholic priest of the less liberal variety, he warned her

about being shunned in the house of God. The Dions believed in God and His wisdom in general, so did not care much for what this particular priest had to say.

The list of Celine's siblings reads like a class roll-call. The oldest of the 14 Dion children is Denise, who was born in 1946. Then there are Clément, Claudette, Liette, Michel, Louise, Jacques, Daniel, Ghislaine, Linda, Manon, and the twins, Paul and Pauline—the latter now employed as president of the Celine Dion Fan Club.

The early family background of the Dions has since been compared, somewhat unfairly, to *The Tin Flute*, a famous novel penned in 1945 by Québec-based author, Gabrielle Roy. Set in the Montreal neighbourhood of Saint-Henri, the novel tells the tale of a working-class mother's struggle to raise a large family against a backdrop of poverty and despair. It is a gritty, family drama of the worthy and historic variety which deals with themes of self-sacrifice and strength in the face of adversity. The book differs from the story of the Dion family in several fundamental respects. The Dions were happy. Their struggle was not futile, and, unlike the father figure in *The Tin Flute*, Adhemar Dion was not unreliable and chronically unemployed.

At school, teachers noticed that the youngest Dion girl seemed withdrawn. Celine did not readily participate in group activities and remained quiet. Whenever she was involved in any boisterous horseplay in the school yard, she took what was meted out by the rougher kids and made no attempt to retaliate. She was slight of build, pale, and shy.

'I could never answer anything at school anyway,' recalls Celine. 'Even when I pass a school today, I hate it for the kids who are there. School was taking me away from my family and friends and my destiny. Every day I would run home from school as fast as I could. I couldn't wait to come back to the basement and hear them rehearse every day.'

Apart from her childhood friend and neighbor, Isobelle Duclos, Celine remembers that outside her family, 'I didn't want to play with the other kids.'

The teachers grew concerned, and informed the local social services department. When the social workers called, they found a house filled with happy kids and hardworking, loving parents. There was the sound of music all around. Mother was baking

OPPOSITE: *Out of the limelight Celine relaxes.*

bread. The visitors were given tea and a sample of fresh, home-baked bread, and saw for themselves just how contented the young Celine was in her home, playing and singing with her brothers and sisters. They witnessed the family dynamic at work and realized that Celine, as the the youngest child, was (as in many families) spoiled and treated with the love and affection of all the rest of the family. They were quick to note that, far from having a problem with her home environment, Celine was only miserable when she was away from it. This was because she missed her brothers and sisters and counted the minutes until she could be with them again around the huge kitchen table—or down in the basement jamming and singing to her heart's content. The social services quickly conceded that their visit was unnecessary and left.

'I was the baby of the family, very spoiled, just like I am now. Social services freaked and said they'd made a mistake,' Celine says. She realizes that, 'It was a great childhood.'

The basement of the family house had become her playground. Here was where the family rehearsed, and the room was filled with musical instruments and equipment. Celine was never really interested in toys and dolls or joining kids to play and pass the time in the street; the basement was her treasure trove of imagination, and the many different instruments were her toys. As soon as she realized what music could do for her and what it had done for her family—in terms of togetherness, expression, emotion and feeling, as well as money—all Celine wanted to do was sing—to express, impress, and bring pleasure to herself and others in the process.

Fellow Canadian superstar, Rita McNeil, one of the country's biggest-selling artists, has said perceptively, 'Music is a big part of Canada. There's not a home where no one plays an instrument, and there's a lot of heritage from Scottish traditions, French culture, and native indians, so it's unique. We do have a very strong identity, but it's hard when you're so close to the States.'

Rita McNeil forms but one link in a long chain of famous Canadian singers and songwriters that stretches back to the early sixties, people like Gordon Lightfoot, Leonard Cohen, Neil Young, Joni Mitchell, and more recently k d lang and Alanis Morissette. The music of Canada has always been an integral part of its culture and national heritage. Bob Dylan once remarked that little can be said about the history of Canada and its people that is not sincerely summed up in Gordon Lightfoot's clas-

sic song, 'Canadian Railroad Trilogy'. Of all Canadian performers who have crossed over into the international market, it is Lightfoot who remains the most steadfast in his Canadian essence, re-inventing the traditional folk approach and creating songs of great beauty and honesty. All these great Canadian artists paved the way for the future of Celine Dion. They were the navvies that laid her yellow brick road, the workers on her railroad of dreams.

All little Celine Dion dreamed about was her singing and where it could take her when she was able to pursue it at professional level. When she convinced her mother that this burning ambition was deep-rooted and genuine, Thérèse made every effort to help her on to that path. She knew that if Celine said she wanted to be a singer, she meant it. After all, she had seen the life and lived the life, sharing it with her parents and brothers and sisters.

'I slept on the floor of every dance hall in Québec,' Celine says. She remembers being taken along with the family to performances: 'I would sleep under mum's coat.'

Celine also remembers that one day, after she had declared her intention to follow her destiny as a singer, her mother very matter-of-factly said, 'You want to be a singer? I want you to do it professionally, with your own songs.'

Thérèse had seen many other youngsters try to make it in show business and realized that talent alone was not enough to seal a success. There has to be support, management, a record deal, and songs that are special in some way. She spent time writing the lyrics for a song and suggested that Celine get together with one of her brothers to compose the music.

'My mum is the person that I look up to,' maintains Celine to this day. 'She's my personal idol.'

Thérèse Dion did not want her young daughter to do the usual circuits of singing in smoky bars and night clubs. If she was to have a professional singing career, it would start out in a professional way. The Dions needed to get Celine's phenomenal vocal talent heard by a manager or producer who would give professional guidance right from the beginning. To do this they needed a demo tape of the song they had written together.

In January 1981 her mother and her brother, Jacques, wrote and arranged a new song specially for Celine's first demo recording. The song was given the, then appro-

priate, title, 'Ce n'était qu'un rêve', which translates as 'Nothing but a Dream'. They recorded the song using their basement as a make-shift studio.

Thérèse packed up the tape in a box tied with red ribbon, hoping to make it stand out, and enclosed the note, 'This is a twelve-year-old with a fantastic voice. Please listen to her. We want her to be like Ginette Reno.' The tape was then sent to René Angelil.

Celine's mother had chosen Angelil after checking the credits on the sleeve of an album by the Québec star, Reno. He was listed as producer, and, as Reno was Celine's heroine and a firm favourite with the whole Dion family, he seemed the obvious first choice. He was well known and respected in Montreal for managing Ginette Reno and also for discovering the child star, René Simard. He had also had a career as a performer himself.

While Celine and her family awaited a response, the box containing the demo tape sat on Angelil's desk, its red ribbon still tied. Angelil's time was, reportedly, taken up with a dispute over Reno's departure from his management to that of her boyfriend, a chef. After successfully managing and guiding Reno's career for many years, he was said to be upset and depressed by the split.

After two weeks had passed, Celine's brother Michel phoned Angelil to urge him to listen to the tape. He told Angelil that he knew he had not listened to it yet, because he would have called the Dions if he had. Five minutes or so later, the phone rang in the Dion household, and Angelil, recognizing considerable talent, requested a meeting with the young singer straight away.

Angelil recalls his first meeting with Celine Dion, 'You wouldn't say she was a cute child, but she had these incredible brown eyes. I asked her to pretend she was in front of 2,000 people. When I handed her a pen to use as a microphone, she closed her eyes and she was there. I had goose bumps listening to her voice, so full of feeling, and older than her years. In the end I was crying.'

There and then, the decision was made. Angelil insisted that he have full control over managing Celine's career. Celine's mother trusted Angelil. Celine trusted her mother's intuition. A deal was signed.

OPPOSITE: *The same incredible brown eyes that enraptured René Angelil when he first met the child Celine.*

*R*ené Angelil, then 38, dropped out from law studies to devote himself full-time to managing and building the career of the 13-year-old Celine. He also dropped all his other clients. He had faith in Celine's potential. He knew that she had everything she needed to succeed: the voice, the talent, the discipline, and the ambition. As Angelil said, 'If you don't have discipline, and if you're not a hard worker, forget it.'

He saw very quickly that Celine was more than capable and also that she had had the full support of her family behind her from a very early age. He decided to concentrate entirely on nurturing this talent, a talent which is rarely seen. 'You hear a voice like that every 10 years,' Angelil enthused, 'so when you hear it, if you're smart, you work hard to have the world know your artist.'

To begin with, he found that his own conviction and enthusiasm did not rub off on any record label executives, who gave little or no consideration to the idea of releas-

I live in song

ing an album by a 12-year-old girl. Undaunted, Angelil took out a mortgage on his house to bankroll the project. In fact, he produced not one but two Celine Dion albums, with the encouragement of his colleagues, Denys Burgeron, who headed local record distribution company, Trans-Canada Disques, and song-writer Eddy Marnay, a French lyricist.

In November 1981, in time for Christmas, Celine released a double debut of two full-length albums on Angelil's Québec-based Super Étoiles label.

La voix du bon dieu, though sung by a child, was not a record for children but was aimed astutely at the adult market, comprising ballads charged with emotion and sentiment, whereas *Céline Dion chante Noël*, which was a collection of traditional Yuletide carols and folk songs, was aimed at the family market. Angelil's faith in the wide

OPPOSITE: *An intimate celebration with husband-manager Angelil.*

18

appeal of Celine's talents proved to be firmly founded, and the gamble paid off, with sales of the two albums for the Christmas season alone exceeding an estimated 30,000 copies. Angelil's house was safe.

Not far into 1982, Celine signed to the Saisons record label, a subsidiary of Trans-Canada. It was already obvious from the reception of her two debut albums that her talent and appeal was bigger than Québec, and the new deal covered all of Canada.

This deal also led to a spin-off signing with EMI-Pathe-Marconi via France-based producer, Claude Pascal. This second deal brought with it access to the superior studio facilities in Paris and to the wider, European French-speaking market. In fact, Dion's reputation was spreading even further afield, and she was awarded a gold medal at the Yamaha World Song Contest in Tokyo in 1982. Over the ensuing four years Celine was to release seven albums in Québec and another two in France.

During this period Celine also became a regular performer on the stages of Québec.

Her live appearances at professional venues began with a series of five low-key concerts during the summer of 1983. Within three years she was appearing at top-notch venues across Québec, and in May 1985 appeared at La Place des Arts in Montreal in a concert which was recorded and immortalized as the live album *Céline Dion en concert.*

Though these earlier recordings are in a different style from her more recent work, they are an interesting and telling catalogue of her continuing development. The 1982 release, *Tellement j'ai d'amour,* was already demonstrating a greater confidence than had been evident in her two first albums.

The following year saw the release of two more albums. *Chantes et contes de noël* was another seasonal offering marketed to appeal to the audience that had bought *Céline Dion chante noël* the previous year. *Les chemins de ma maison* is a more mature collection of songs, with a finesse that allows more facets of Celine's developing talent to shine through.

Her fourth single, 'D'amour ou d'amitié', was a surprise success, selling an estimated 300,000 copies in Canada alone, with a further 400,000 sales in Europe. This figure equaled the combined sales total of the first three singles, which was already an impressive statistic. 'D'amour ou d'amitié' earned her a gold disc in France, making her the first Canadian ever to achieve this accolade.

During this period, at age 15, Celine dropped out of school (with her mother's approval), having yet to acquire any useful grasp of English. She has no regrets about not completing her full term at high school, 'because I was not very comfortable at school. I hated it. I couldn't learn. I was dreaming, I couldn't concentrate, because I was learning stuff I knew I was not going to use. School is not for everybody, I believe, and I didn't like it. I'm going to the school of life and I'm learning much more.'

1984 was marked by two historic performances. 16-year-old Celine first sang before an audience of 65,000 at Montreal's Olympic Stadium for a special performance for the visiting Pope, John-Paul II. She later gave a headline concert at Montreal's famous Olympia Theatre. Her concerts around this period were entirely in French, with the occasional exception of a single English song, 'Flashdance: What a Feeling', originally made famous by Irene Cara. Celine remembers that the song was always well received, with audiences clapping along and dancing, but she did not understand a word of what she was singing.

During 1984 Celine began voice studies in Paris with the renowned tutor, Tosca Marmor. This was her only formal training.

At 17 she felt that she had outgrown her child-star persona and wanted to be more than la p'tite Québecoise. It is at this point that many stars who have achieved success early—the Debbie Gibsons and Tiffanies of the pop world—drop from view, only resurfacing in some parallel career on stage or screen years later.

Celine Dion, with her five-octave soprano, had already had an enviable career. She was famous and wealthy enough to have bought her parents a lake-side home just outside Monteal in 1986. The house overlooks the popular Sainte-Anne-des-Lacs ski resort. Celine decorated the place herself in white throughout. Between tours she would spend time there with her mother, father, visiting relatives, and her cat, Isis. She also enjoyed forgetting her slick designer image and relaxing in jeans, tying back her hair, and going for drives in the country in her Jeep Cherokee.

On the advice of René Angelil, Celine suspended her career for an 18 month period, during which she collected herself and considered the future. She also had her front teeth capped, restyled her hair, and assembled an entirely new wardrobe for herself.

Her relaunch came with *Incognito* in 1987, an eight-track album released as her debut for major label, Sony. It was immediately apparent that Celine had abruptly shifted up a gear. She had redesigned and remodeled herself with a chic, sexy image, and the music reflected the more mature, adult approach. The mainstay of her previous work had been ballads with traditional, sometimes folksy backing. Now she launched headlong into a slicker pop format with a heavier beat and bigger sound, her more forceful vocal style backed up and swept along by saxophone refrains. Sony's press release announcing the new-style Dion summed it up with the line, 'When youth, beauty and talent come together in one package, the results are truly explosive.'

Celine and Angelil must have been apprehensive about how her new image would affect her popularity. It was, in many respects, a make or break period. The shift from the homely domestic appeal of la p'tite Québecoise to this sleek confidence was a dramatic one which ran the risk of alienating many of her followers.

There was, of course, a spattering of bad reviews, and there were critics who saw her change of image as some sort of sell-out, a betrayal of her roots, but to Celine's delight, her career seemed to pick up where it had left off without missing a beat. She

embarked on a rigorous schedule of support appearances in and around Montreal which sold out 42 consecutive concerts in advance.

The album, *Incognito*, her ninth full-length, original LP, was very well received in Québec, and went on to sell 200,000 copies in Canada.

Although Celine's record sales remained impressive in Québec, the image change did not boost sales to any great extent outside her already consolidated territory. Her fan-base in France still paid attention to this rising star, though the more general public continued to be indifferent, and resistance from the English-speaking market remained impenetrable. The appetite for Celine in Europe was still easily satisfied with small-scale releases, and her European label, Carrere (a subsidiary of Sony) took to releasing small runs of Celine's singles solely to test the market.

Even with nine albums to her credit, Celine was little known outside Québec and France. This was to change when two Swiss songwriters, Nella Martinetti and Attila Sereftug, approached Celine with a song they had written as the 1988 Eurovision Song Contest entry for Switzerland. The song was 'Ne partez pas sans moi' ('Don't Leave Without Me').

Although Celine had not heard of the Eurovision Song Contest, she jumped at the chance to reach a wider European audience, and flew to Dublin, Ireland to perform the song for a television audience of around 600 million.

'I felt honored to be representing Switzerland,' she says of the event. 'We had a great time; we met lots of people. It was like traveling Europe without traveling too much.'

René Angelil gambled on the outcome: 'I bet everything I had on me at the time for Celine to win. I still have the betting ticket!'

The Eurovision winner for 1988 was Switzerland! Celine had triumphed, and suddenly Europe knew who she was. As usual with a Eurovision winner, the single sold well in most European countries and stirred up general interest in this young singer with a remarkable voice. Often Eurovision contestants are small-time performers or newcomers, so the press was pleasantly surprised to find that Celine Dion had a nine-album history behind her.

Carrere made use of this kick-start and promptly launched into a schedule of releas-

OPPOSITE: *Celine at the 1988 Eurovision Song Contest, where a win brought recognition in Europe.*

es to capitalize on Celine's raised profile and continue the momentum. It was the dawning of a new Dion era, both professionally and personally.

It was while in Dublin that René and Celine exchanged their first kiss, realizing that the love they had always felt for each other had developed beyond the platonic and was leaning toward the romantic. Their relationship as manager and artist had always been founded on total trust and mutual respect. A solid enough basis for a professional association and also the perfect foundation for deeper feelings.

Celine Dion had dated only one boy seriously, and only for a matter of weeks. She had found that she was too involved with her career for a relationship. She felt that she could not give half of herself to a romantic entanglement and half to her singing. Singing was what defined her, and it required her attention 100 per cent. She had joked in interviews, when journalists speculated on her love life, that it had just not worked out and that she would have to find a boyfriend who was also in showbiz.

Although the Eurovision win pushed up record sales for Celine in French-speaking countries, it failed to make much impact on England, and made virtually none on the lucrative American market. Celine realized that as long as she remained a Francophone artist—singing only in French—she would always be marginalized. She remembers how much of a struggle it was doing press interviews with English journalists when she won the Eurovision: 'I was always sitting on the edge of my chair, understanding three words out of every five.'

The record company could only coax many of the journalists to interview Celine Dion if they promised them an additional act to talk to. It was more than apparent to Celine that she had to learn English to break into new territories. Now that she needed to speak English in order to pursue her dream to its heights, she proved that she was bright enough to master the language with apparent ease. Within two years of the Eurovision Song Contest, as soon as her schedule allowed, she went back to school to take a Berlitz short course.

The course was a six-month intensive, five days a week, nine till five every day. To begin with, Celine was a little lost because the lessons were almost entirely presented in English. By the end of the course, however, she was competent enough to consider a new branch of her career: in English. She also knew that many of her fans were French-speaking, and that a good section of her audience shared her Québec roots.

She would not forget them. She saw English as an additional direction in which to take her music, not an alternative. She also had the insight to realize that the feel and sound of the two languages suited different themes and emotions; one was not better than the other.

There was some backlash, as there always is when a person achieves any notable degree of success. This was typified at the 1990 Felix Awards when Celine was voted Anglophone Artist of the Year. The Felix Awards are the top music awards in Québec, with 46 categories for French-language and just one for English-language performance. By placing her in the Anglophone category, the awards committee had effectively excluded her from all the others, even though she still released material in French. Celine took to the stage at the Awards Ceremony not to accept but to refuse the Felix, stating that she was proud to be Québecoise and was not an Anglophone artist.

ABOVE: *Celine celebrates her 1988 Eurovision win in a big way.*

*I*n 1990, with a decade-long career behind her, Celine Dion performed before the visiting royals, Charles and Diana, Prince and Princess of Wales, at a special concert in Ottawa. That same year she released her first album in the English language, *Unison.*

The album was recorded in Los Angeles, New York, and London, with song writing input from David Foster, Stan Meissner, and Aldo Nova. David Foster and Tom Keane produced the Los Angeles sessions, Andy Goldmark oversaw the New York recording, and Christopher Neil was in charge of the London production. As is usual with a Celine Dion album, the tracks recorded at each studio were already complete and on tape before Celine herself arrived to lay down the vocals.

It was a project she knew had massive potential but also embodied a large risk. The bigger the possible success, the bigger the possible failure. She remembers having recurring nightmares with classic insecurity ingredients. In one such dream, which she

Love has no age

reportedly suffered six times, she recalls standing on a narrow ledge high up on a sky-scraper looking down at swarms of ambulances and police cars. As a police officer reaches out to her, she either falls or jumps and only wakes the instant before impact with the sidewalk. 'I have to pretend I am a strong person,' she has confessed, 'but really I am so afraid of making a mistake.'

Her fears were further escalated during the promotional tour for the album when at a concert in Sherbrooke, Québec, her voice failed her. It was a special performance at a record retailers' convention, and—although Celine would have been equally upset by her voice failing before an audience of die-hard fans—on stage before a hall full of industry representatives the experience must have been especially devastating.

She sought the help and advice of Wilbur Gould, a famous throat specialist in New

OPPOSITE: *Celine puts heart and soul into laying down vocals in the recording studio.*

York. He advised her to rest her larynx and vocal chords for three weeks. She followed this advice and took a vacation on a beach where the air was clear and humid, and refrained from speaking. The only mode of communication she allowed herself was mime or notes written on a reporters' pad.

From that time onward, Celine has followed the advice of voice specialists and always takes every precaution to ensure that her voice remains in prime condition for her concerts and studio work. She had never smoked and did not often drink alcohol, so abstinence from those substances has been no hardship. She always travels with two humidifiers, one for hotel rooms and one for the dressing room or studio. On the day of a performance she will only talk when absolutely necessary and observes a vow of silence from late afternoon onward. Sometimes before a recording session she will not talk for days. She does at least 35 minutes of vocal exercises every day.

After a show, Celine has a light supper, as she eats little or nothing before a performance. She then goes to bed and sleeps for up to 14 hours, waking up around three

o'clock in the afternoon, when she will have a combined breakfast and lunch. At approximately five o'clock she does her vocal exercises for up to an hour, before taking a high-humidity shower. She avoids talking until she arrives at the venue for the sound check. She drinks tea or warm water with honey and lemon, and uses a natural remedy elixir for her throat.

The trials and tribulations leading up to the release of *Unison* were proven worthwhile. Released across Canada and the USA in April 1990, the album made the hoped for impact.

It was a completely new direction for Dion. Apart from being her first album venture into English, the music was also unlike anything that had gone before. However, no apprehension was evident, and Celine's vocals were bold and confident. The record was an instant success across Canada and took up temporary residence in the Top 10 of the national album charts. In the USA it was not so warmly received, and it took several singles before the epic ballad, 'Where Does My Heart Beat Now?', broke

ABOVE: *An impish Celine well on the route to international fame.*

through and remained in the charts for 24 weeks, climbing to the number four position.

The remainder of the year and on into 1992 was taken up with extensive promotion and touring to cement the success in the English-speaking market which up to that time had been so elusive. It was, then, a brave move to return to French language for the next album.

Celine chose to make an entire album based on the compositions of Luc Plamondon, a respected Québec song writer who is best known for his rock opera, *Starmania*. The album, *Dion chante Plamondon*, confirmed her loyalty to her long-standing Québec fan-base and earned her a gold disc there. In France, where the release was given the alternative title of *Des mots qui sonnet*, the album went platinum.

During 1991 Celine Dion also made her acting debut on television in the French-Canadian mini-series, *Les fleurs sur la neige*. In this hard-hitting drama she portrayed a sixteen-year-old victim of abuse. The series was based on a real case in which a girl took her parents to court. The role would have been difficult for an established actress, but for a newcomer it must certainly have been a great challenge. Celine admitted that, 'It was a difficult role,' though it did whet her appetite for acting more in the future, and she was, 'very happy with the results'.

Simply titled, *Celine Dion*, the 1992 English-language follow-up to *Unison* maintained its predecessor's success. Celine was awarded her first gold record in America for the album, which sold half a million copies in its first six months of sales. Two singles taken from the LP also performed well in the USA national charts. 'If You Asked Me To' stuck at number one for three weeks, and 'Love Can Move Mountains' managed to make a dent on the black music charts with a brash, hybrid sound that combined elements from blues and gospel.

Celine Dion was echoing in her career sentiments that Gordon Lightfoot expressed in his 1971 song, 'Nous vivons ensemble'. In this classic song, Lightfoot sings one section in English and another in French, and addresses the issues of Québec's cultural identity within Canada. In the lyric he recommends that, 'we've got to live together,' and that we should 'learn all about the other man's song', suggesting that music and pride in the Canadian heritage can unify as well as define, and that music with honest expression can help people overcome their differences, or at least understand them.

The subject of independence for Québec is cause for great debate in the province. When Celine Dion began recording in English, she laid herself open to attack from right-wing separatists who believe that French-speaking Québec should be independent of Canada. Some saw her use of English as a form of betrayal. Even the minor fact that an accent was dropped from the spelling of her name on album covers stirred up some dissent.

Although Celine Dion does have an opinion on the subject, she keeps it to herself for both commercial and moral reasons. 'I think everybody has an opinion, and I respect everybody's opinion,' she has commented, 'but I think politics has no feeling, and it destroys a lot of the soul.'

She believes that her fans understand why she sings in English: 'They know I'm doing it sincerely, because I want it. I love it. I really love to sing in English and in French. I think there will always be a little something extra in my French singing, because I am a Francophone first of all, in my blood. But English is the language of

ABOVE: *Celine: keeping her opinions to herself, but always sincere*

OPPOSITE: *A glamorous amd sexy Celine, her child-star image far behind.*

music; it stands by itself, and it's natural. French is so romantic—I can't choose!'

Yet anyone who achieves success attracts their share of vindictive detractors. Celine Dion has borne the brunt of some rather illogical political posturing. Because she comes from the working-class, rural, Catholic tradition, with its typically large families, she has been held up as a symbol of a past Québec that many would rather not be associated with.

Some sections of the Québec press took advantage of any opportunity to attempt to belittle her growing success, stooping to rumor mongering. There was innuendo regarding her relationship with her manager and suggestions that she was anorexic. Both accusations were vehemently denied at the time, with legal proceedings where necessary.

It was, of course, vastly unfair of such factions to victimize an easy target solely because she was becoming a public figure. In one television interview with talk-show host, Lise Payette, Celine was reduced to tears when commenting on the way some sections of the public had treated her in her own home province of Québec. The inter-

ABOVE: *Celine in 1993, the year of her first headline US tour.*

view proved to be a turning point of sorts, and from that point on her success has gone from strength to strength. Soon afterwards anyone who criticized her ran the risk of shooting themselves in the foot; it was simply not done. Celine earned the respect of her entire country as an ambassador for Québec and Canada. The French-language media of Québec were soon referring to her as 'notre Celine nationale' ('our national Celine').

For many, Celine Dion has come to symbolize the difficult balance between old Québec's traditions and insular attitude, and modern Québec's desire to be open to the world and the possibilities presented by multi-cultural interaction.

The big, truly international break for Celine came when she was selected to sing the title song for Disney's animated feature film, *Beauty And The Beast*, a duet to be performed with Peabo Bryson.

Celine Dion was surprised to be approached by Disney to perform this high-profile theme song. She was not very familiar with the quintessentially American mega-corporation, Disney, 'I grew up in a big family,' she explained; 'I didn't grow up with cartoons.' She had come to the attention of Disney executives through her single, 'Where Does My Heart Beat Now?', which received extensive radio play in the USA.

She accepted the invitation to go and see the full-length cartoon adaptation of the fairy tale and found herself enraptured by its magic: 'It was so beautiful!' She was then more than happy to accept Disney's other invitation, to sing the title song with Peabo Bryson.

Christopher Neil, who was to produce the song for Disney, flew to Los Angeles to present it to Celine. He played it to her, and her immediate response was, 'I want the song!'

Shortly afterwards, Neil and another producer, Alto Nova, came to some nearby studios in Morin Heights, a town 50 km north of Montreal, in the Laurentian mountains. There they recorded the song that would go on to win a Grammy and an Academy Award. 'I consider today that I've been part of a classic,' Celine has said. 'I've been very lucky; it started my whole career, and it's going to be with me for the rest of my life.'

Celine was able to celebrate her 24th birthday with a live performance of 'Beauty and The Beast' with Peobo Bryson at the Academy Awards ceremony for an estimat-

ed two-billion-strong television audience across the world.

The following year, 1993, was to see her international stardom step up a few more notches, taking her record sales along with it. It was to mark her first tour of the USA as a headline act. This was a prospect that greatly excited Celine. She put every ounce of effort she could muster into the preparation for the tour, knowing that it could cement her new-found success. She was going to make sure she reaped the potential benefits. For an artist who is often criticized for being too willing to hand over control of her career and image to others, Celine Dion threw herself into the tasks of planning and designing the tour. She had a hand in nearly every aspect from sets to costume, from lighting rigs to sound systems. She recalls lying awake at night thinking everything through well in advance: 'I couldn't sleep, putting ideas on paper! From the beginning, I built everything.'

It is her time on stage that is the aspect of her career Celine most enjoys. 'The stage is magic,' she has said, 'You feel all the artists that went before you. It's very difficult

ABOVE: *Celine joyfully accepts a 1993 Grammy Award.*

OPPOSITE: *A radiant Celine at her 1994 wedding to René Angelil.*

to explain, but when you are born to become a performer and you're on stage, you feel something very special.'

In 1993, in the midst of a rise to new heights of fame for Celine, a family tragedy struck that deeply affected her. A niece, Karine Menard died. Karine was the daughter of Celine's sister Liette, and had been born in 1977 with cystic fibrosis, a progressive and debilitating disease which affects the whole body, particularly the respiratory and digestive systems. Celine visited regularly, often taking Karine on outings. She enjoyed her many trips to the malls with her niece, taking along with her all the necessary medical accessories, such as oxygen tanks.

On Celine's final visit to see Karine, her niece was worse than usual. Grandmother Dion, was massaging Karine's feet to encourage failing circulation. Celine sang softly and held Karine in her arms until her eyes closed for the last time. Later that year Celine Dion became a patron of the Canadian Cystic Fibrosis Foundation.

1993 was also a year of great personal happiness. One night Celine was sitting down to a relaxed dinner with René when he was suddenly overcome with emotion. Celine

ABOVE: *Great personal happiness: Celine and René joined in marriage.*

was concerned and asked him if he was OK. With tears in his eyes he assured her that all was fine, and produced an instantly recognizable, small box—the kind of presentation box that contains expensive rings. But instead of handing it over, for a while he just looked at it and cried.

When Celine later recounted these events to the nation on *The Rosie O'Donnell Show*, the hostess joked with her that he may have been thinking of the price tag, and that was what brought him to tears. But Celine had been charmed and had had no hesitation in accepting his wonderful gesture.

Celine must have realized just how much her manager and mentor meant to her the previous year, when on May 7 1992, during a visit to Los Angeles, Angelil suffered a heart attack. The attack was almost certainly brought on by the excessive work that he had continually piled upon himself. When he became ill the roles were reversed, and Celine took charge and got him to hospital in a taxi. He recovered relatively quickly, though the scare had its affect on Celine, 'René is the engine of my life,' she later told reporters; 'without him, I feel like a car without an engine; there are things I simply can't figure out.'

The year of 1993 was capped with the release of the album *The Colour Of My Love* in November. In the liner notes for the album, Celine declares her love for manager-producer, René, and dedicates it to him.

The album was a mixed bag of slick pop ballads and dance-orientated numbers. There is the duet, 'When I Fall In Love', performed with Clive Griffin, which also appears on the soundtrack for the Meg Ryan movie, *Sleepless In Seattle*. There is a darker feel to the track, 'Refuse To Dance', which Celine described as, 'the kind of song Annie Lennox or Madonna would do'.

The first single released from the album was 'The Power Of Love', which was to be Celine Dion's first number one success in the USA. It stayed at the top of the Billboard chart for four weeks and inspired enough confidence in the market to warrant a short tour of the USA during 1994.

The wedding of René Angelil, 52, and Celine Dion, 26, was a spectacular occasion. Some would call it a fairy-tale wedding.

On December 17 1994, 500 family and friends gathered for the intimate ceremony at the Notre Dame Basilica in Montreal. A motorcade of 17 limousines had brought

the guests, and a fanfare of trumpets heralded the arrival of the groom's car.

The event was the closest thing to a royal wedding that Québec is ever likely to see. The area had been cordoned off to control the crowds, which started to gather eight hours before the service was scheduled. As tradition dictates, the bride arrived half an hour late, in a gleaming, wine-colored Rolls Royce, escorted by twelve state police cars.

The crowds were finally rewarded with a glimpse of their pop princess as she made her way into the church. She wore a white silk bridal gown, detailed with sequins and tiny pearls, with a long train. It had been specially designed by a local designer, Mirella Gentile.

On entering the church, there was a serenade from Celine's brothers and sisters, who sang a specially composed song for the couple. Celine walked down the aisle accompanied by a string orchestra playing the title track from the album, *The Colour Of My Love*, which she had dedicated to her husband-to-be.

'I felt like a princess in a fairy tale,' she told the gathering of reporters. 'It was magic, the ceremony of my dreams. What I had always hoped for. I remember saying 'yes' and that's all!'

After the vows had been exchanged, the newly-weds and their guests moved on to the reception at a nearby hotel. The reception hall was decked out with cascades of roses, and the sweeping staircase was strewn with flower petals.

For Celine it was the perfect day: 'I wanted to have a fairy-tale wedding—I was having a fairy tale life! Family, husband, career.'

The day was reported as having cost an estimated half a million dollars. The cost of an event of such a scale soon mounts up. There is the hiring of venues, the food, the dress, the cars and drivers, the flowers, the police presence, and crowd control in the city streets. Even with the 500 guests, the event was basically for family and close friends only, but with nine sisters and five brothers—all older and married with children, some of *them* now married with children themselves—plus uncles, aunts and cousins . . . 'We have 35 nieces and nephews,' explained Celine; 'most of them are married, and they have children. I'm a grand-aunt!'

OPPOSITE: *Celine and René leave the Basilica after their 'fairy-tale' wedding.*

For a gathering of this size, the wedding cake has to be huge, and it was. Celine wanted something special, and profiteroles are one of her favourite sweets. The catering company devised a wedding cake consisting of a 12-foot-high pyramid made out of 2,000 of the caramel filled pastries.

The happy couple declined wedding gifts, instead requesting that the throngs of well-wishers make donations to the Canadian Cystic Fibrosis Foundation research fund—donations which totaled around $200,000.

For the honeymoon, they chose to have a quiet three-week break from interviews and public appearances in Florida. Their plans were curtailed when the single, 'Think Twice' became a hit in the UK, and at the request of Sony they flew to England for Celine to appear on British television's *Top Of The Pops*.

*I*n 1995 Celine made French musical history with her next album *D'eux*, also known outside France as *The French Album*. It was written by Jean-Jaques Goldman, who has been called 'the Bruce Springstein of France' and is one of the country's leading and most consistent stars. Celine, who knew him only by reputation and from having heard his music on the radio during visits to France, was surprised and delighted when she heard from more than one source that he had expressed a desire to work with her.

Phone calls were made and a lunch meeting was set up for herself, Goldman, and, of course, Angelil. Her delight was all the greater when Goldman told her that he wanted to write an entire album for her. 'I was pretty amazed,' admits Celine. 'He doesn't write a whole album for anybody but himself.'

Celine, who must have been aware of the man's stature in France, was flattered. A teaming of Dion and Goldman would certainly attract attention, and the

A forever person

quality of his song-writing was its own testimony.

Celine then flew off to Japan for a series of appearances and concerts. She provided the title song for a 10-part Japanese television series, entitled *Koibito Yo* (*My Dear Lover*). The song was 'To Love You More', and though it was sung in English it proved far more popular than expected. When released as a single, it sold one and a half million copies, taking it to the number one position in Japan's national singles chart. This made Celine Dion the first non-Japanese act to reach the top of the Japanese charts for 12 years. The song was produced by David Foster, who wrote it with Junior Miles (the latter being the *nom de plume* of Seagram Chairman, Edgar Bronfman Jr).

Ironically, the last foreign act to have reached number one in Japan had been Irene Cara with 'Flashdance: What A Feeling', the only English-language song Celine

OPPOSITE: *An international artist: Celine at the 1995 Grammy Awards.*

used in her own early live concerts.

On her return to Paris soon afterwards, she met Jean-Jaques Goldman again to hear some of the material he had come up with for her. He presented a brace of songs which touched Celine's deepest core. She described hearing his words and music as being brought face to face with her own emotions.

The resultant album was 1995's *D'eux*. The album contained songs that tackled difficult subjects. The track 'L'Amour Existe Encore' addresses the subject of love in a social climate of AIDS, and 'Ziggy' tells the story of a young girl in love with a gay man. Celine sings an English version of 'Ziggy' on the 1992 soundtrack compilation album, *Tycoon*.

D'eux debuted in the French chart at number one. It remained at the top of the charts for an unprecedented 44 weeks, garnering favorable reviews in the press and comparisons with Edith Piaf. It was awarded the highly-prized French Medal of Arts, and went on in just seven weeks to become the best-selling album ever in France. It also became the first ever French-language album to win a gold disc in the UK. It

ABOVE: *Celine Dion: many times a laureate.*

remained tenaciously in the number one slot in France until it was eventually displaced, a good part of a year later, by Celine Dion's next album, *Falling Into You*.

In the meantime Celine contributed to a special CD to raise money for and awareness of the Canadian Breast Cancer Research Initiative. The CD album was titled *In Between Dances* and was the brainchild of Vancouver singer Jacki Ralph Jamieson, who had moderate fame in the seventies as lead singer with The Bells. She had been fighting breast and ovarian cancer for five years when she came up with the idea of the album.

The CD ended up as a 17-track compilation which brought together 22 of Canada's most famous female vocalists. In addition to Jamieson and Dion, there were K D Lang, Sarah McLaughlan, Jann Arden, Alannah Myles, Patricia Conroy, Holly Cole, Sara Craig, Michelle Wright, Loreen McKennitt, Susan Aglukark, The Rankin Family, Quartette, and Rita McNeil. The track that Celine Dion donated was 'Send Me A Lover'.

Celine also contributed to another compilation album in 1995. This time it was a

ABOVE: *Celine in concert at Wembley Arena.*

tribute to Carole King which took the form of a reworking of King's classic album, *Tapestry*, with contemporary artists influenced by the singer-songwriter providing cover versions of each track. The album was entitled *Tapestry Revisited*, and Celine Dion chose to cover '(You Make Me Feel Like a) Natural Woman'.

The success of *D'eux* in France was echoed throughout the world when its successor, *Falling Into You*, became the biggest-selling album of 1996, reaching the top of the charts in no less than 11 countries. The record's phenomenal achievement earned Celine recognition around the globe, and the music industries of various countries honored her with their most prestigious awards. At the World Music Awards in Monte Carlo, she picked up three awards: Best-Selling Canadian Artist, World's Best-Selling Pop Artist, and World's Best-Selling Overall Artist. At home in Canada she picked up four Juno Awards: Best-Selling Album Foreign or Domestic, International Achievement Award, Female Vocalist of The Year, and (for her album, *Live à Paris*) Best Selling Francophone Album. *Falling Into You* also won both Album of the Year

ABOVE: *An elegant Celine attends the 1995 World Music Awards in Monte Carlo.*

OPPOSITE: *Celine in party mood.*

and Best Pop Album at the 39th annual Grammy Awards.

As always, Angelil was prepared to capitalize on the album's success and the profile of its single 'Because You Loved Me', which was also gathering associated coverage due to its inclusion on the soundtrack of the Robert Redford and Michelle Pfeiffer vehicle, *Up Close And Personal*. The film was a box-office success in the USA and earned a most respectable $11 million at the box office during its first weekend on release. Angelil used the opportunity to arrange a rigorous schedule of appearances for Celine.

Success begets success. For example, during one week in March of 1996 Celine appeared on national television for *The Grammy Awards*, *The Tonight Show with Jay Leno*, and *The Blockbuster Awards*, in addition to smaller TV shows. She also gave several radio interviews and was prominent presence in the advertizing campaign for *Up Close And Personal*.

The single 'Because You Loved Me' swiftly climbed the USA Billboard charts and reached number one, a position which it held on to for six consecutive weeks. *Falling Into You* went straight into the national album charts at the number two position.

ABOVE: *A jubilant Celine accepts a 1995 World Music Award.*

OPPOSITE: *Soon to sing at the 1996 Olympic Games, Celine celebrates in the arms of Angelil.*

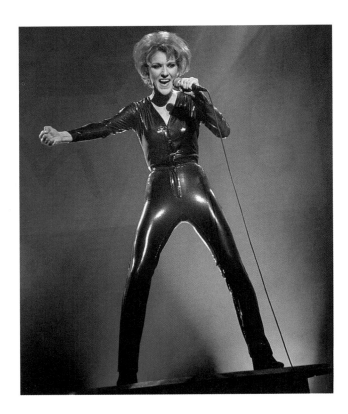

Dion's success in the USA market was certainly consolidated, and she was well on her way to becoming a household name.

The Dion management had settled on an impressive short list of production talent for the sessions for *Falling Into You*. They commissioned David Foster, Aldo Nova, and Todd Rundgren, as well as Jim Steinman, to produced the bulk of material for the album. Steinman is the producer and song-writer famous for Meat Loaf's *Bat Out Of Hell* album, plus a string of hits for the likes of Bonnie Tyler and soft metal merchants, Heart. Celine was thrilled to be working with yet another legend. 'Jim Steinman is incredible!' she enthused. 'Every song to him is like a movie.' She did not mind that he drove her hard and was extremely demanding.

The sort of regimen that Celine is used to when recording, is spending around three hours on each song, performing it maybe eight times. With Steinman, she found herself being asked to sing the songs through 20, sometimes 30, times. She described him as a workaholic and was amazed at how he could select just what he wanted from each

ABOVE: *A raunchy Celine in concert in 1996.*

track she put down. She was always confident in his ability, and she found it a pleasure to work with someone who was prepared to put so much into the project.

Jim Steinman expressed reciprocal respect for Dion and noted that, although she was completely prepared to re-record and put in the performances that he demanded, she always knew exactly what she wanted from the sessions. He described her as 'aggressive in the sweetest way'.

A potential partnership that did not work out on *Falling Into You* was with Phil Spector, the highly influential producer responsible for the 'wall of sound' recordings made famous in the sixties by acts like the Ronnettes, and Ike and Tina Turner. He has a lengthy list of credits to his name which include, most notably, his work with Scott Walker, the poetic purveyor of cinematically soundscaped ballads of the most awe-inspiring proportions.

Phil Spector had seen Celine Dion perform 'River Deep, Mountain High' on an edition of The Late Show, a song he had originally produced for Ike and Tina Turner. This

ABOVE: *With Angelil at the World Music Awards in 1997, where Celine was a major winner.*

was atypically rock-and-roll-orientated material for Celine, but her impressive rendition was enough to motivate Spector to seek her out and offer his talents. It had been nearly 15 years since Spector had overseen an album for any artist (his last collaboration being *End Of The Century* with The Ramones in 1980).

The performance of 'River Deep, Mountain High' on *The Late Show* had been the result of a challenge laid down by the show's producers. They had invited Celine to appear on the show but had asked that she forgo her usual big ballad and 'try something'. They suggested maybe a rock-and-roll song. Celine had risen to the occasion in choosing to perform a song which would lure its original producer out of his near retirement. The general response to her new direction was good, and the song eventually made it on to the album, but was the only evidence of any connection with Spector.

The involvement of Phil Spector lasted around two months and bore little fruit. He and Celine worked on several tracks which remain unfinished. These recording sessions were apparently on a grand scale, involving a 60-piece orchestra. It seems that Phil Spector's notoriously temperamental personality clashed with nearly all the others involved in the project. This may have been one of the factors that caused the recordings with Spector to over-run, overlapping with Dion's scheduled New York recording sessions.

In a much-quoted statement to the magazine, *Entertainment Weekly*, Spector explains at length the reasons for his fall-out with Dion. He praises the 'extraordinary talents of Ms Celine Dion' but goes on to refer to other people involved as, 'amateurs, students and clones of yours truly', saying that the team seemed only to be interested in recording hits, 'even if they were contrived and repugnant or nothing more than Whitney Houston-Mariah Carey-rejected, sound-alike songs and records'. He goes on to claim that, 'It became apparent that the people around Ms Dion were more interested in controlling the project and the people recording her than making history.' He concludes , 'You don't tell Shakespeare what plays to write, or how to write them. You don't tell Mozart what operas to write, or how to write them. And you certainly don't tell Phil Spector what songs to write, or how to write them; or what records to pro-

OPPOSITE: *A glowing Celine at the Smash Hits Awards*

duce or how to produce them.' Nevertheless, he assures readers that he fully intends to complete the production and mixing of the recordings he made with Celine and release them on his own record label, claiming that they are 'amazing and historic recordings'.

David Foster was reported as saying that he found Spector's attitude, 'a little pompous'. Jim Steinman remained philosophical, claiming gleefully, 'I'm thrilled to be insulted by Phil Spector. He's my god, my idol. To be insulted by Phil Spector is a big honor. If he spits on me, I consider myself purified.' However, Celine Dion, polite and diplomatic as ever, puts it all down to experience and hopes that she will have the chance to work with Spector again, and more fruitfully, in the future, saying, 'I was pretty devastated, because I love the song he wrote. I had a great time with Phil. He had two or three months to deliver three songs. He couldn't do it in this time. And I'm not mad at this. It's OK. I would love to work with him again.'

Falling Into You debuted in the USA Billboard charts at number two and remained

ABOVE: *Celine smiling after the filming of a Bee Gees video.*

OPPOSITE: *Gently radiant, Celine attends the 1996 Billboard Awards.*

there for weeks, just kept from the number one slot by fellow Canadian, Alanis Morissette, with her hard-to-swallow *Jagged Little Pill*. The single 'Because You Loved Me' went rapidly to number one in the single charts and tenaciously held that position for two months.

In Canada the 15-track album was received with great enthusiasm. In one record store in Toronto the CD sold 400 copies in two hours on the day of its release. Sony had shipped 400,000 copies, and were immediately taking re-orders from retailers. With the instant success of her new album and with sales of her previous *The Colour Of My Love* having already topped 12 million, Celine Dion was well on her way to becoming the greatest commercial success that the Canadian music industry has ever spawned.

In April of 1996, a month after the initial release of *Falling Into You* and following an Australian tour, Celine Dion had the honor of being the first artist to perform at the newly completed Molson Centre in Montreal. A sell-out Canadian tour followed.

Celine again lent her talents to a charity album in 1996. The record *For Our Children* Too was aimed at raising funds for and awareness of the Paediatric AIDS Foundation. Dion contributed two songs, 'Brahms Lullaby' and 'Love Lights the World', which also involved input from David Foster, Peabo Bryson, and Color Me Badd.

Although Celine is one of the biggest, fastest-selling international stars in history, both she and her husband still have their roots firmly in the soil of Québec, and choose to live there when their rigorous schedule allows them to stay in one place for more than a week or so.

By 1996 they had opened a chain of 25 restaurants throughout Québec. At a branch of Nickels the clientele can expect to enjoy speciality smoked meats in a fifties-style diner atmosphere.

1996 marked yet another big moment in Celine's making of music history. A definite proponent of the 'follow your dream' philosophy, Celine Dion was an excellent choice to perform a specially composed song at the opening ceremony of the 1996 centenary Olympic Games.

OPPOSITE: *Celine Dion: one of the biggest, fastest-selling stars in music history.*

Entitled 'The Power Of The Dream', the song was written by a trio of industry heavyweights, Kenny 'Babyface' Edmonds, and husband and wife team Linda Thompson and David Foster. David Foster had already worked with Dion as a producer, notably on the two massive singles, 'The Power Of Love' (which earned him a Grammy nomination) and 'Because You Loved Me'. Foster had earned a string of no less than 12 Grammies for his work as composer, producer, performer, and arranger for artists such as Barbra Streisand, Whitney Houston, Natalie Cole, and Madonna. Among these Awards were three for Producer of the Year: one in 1984 for the album *Chicago XVIII*, another in 1992 for Natalie Cole's *Unforgettable*, and a third in 1994 for work on two soundtrack albums, *The Bodyguard* with Whitney Houston and *Sleepless In Seattle* with Celine Dion. Babyface Edmonds, also a multi-Grammy-Award-winner, co-wrote the music for 'The Power of the Dream' with Foster, while Thompson (who was previously married to Olympic athlete Bruce Jenner) provided the lyrics.

The opening ceremony on July 19 was a huge event, witnessed world-wide by a television audience of around six billion. More than 10,000 athletes from 197 delegations competed. Don Mischer, executive producer in charge of organizing the opening and closing ceremonies, described the 'The Power of the Dream' as 'a gripping and emotional ballad that will help create the sense of drama we need to grab the world's attention'. He went on to say, 'We are very fortunate. The world's expectations for the opening ceremony are unbelievably high. Dion's extraordinary voice and the combined talents of everyone involved in the song will make this piece a memorable part of the ceremonies.'

The invitation to perform this special song at the Olympic Games appealed to Celine for obvious reasons. It was both a gift and a public relations opportunity, a chance to ensure that her voice was heard across the world. It was also an honor to be chosen to sing at the Olympic spectacular and to stand in the same arena as athletes who represent excellence and achievement throughout the world. She appreciated 'the sacrifices they made, their dedication and commitment to a single purpose. The hard work they have gone through makes every one of them a hero, just for having

OPPOSITE: *Dion and Streisand: working with Barbra was a 'dream come true'.*

earned the privilege of being on that field for the opening ceremony.' Celine also felt that she had something in common with the competitors: 'I appreciate the importance of discipline in achieving your dream.'

Celine's song-writing relationship with Foster and Thompson was reprised on her next and biggest album to date, *Let's Talk About Love*, which was released around the world on November 8 1997. With its predecessor *Falling Into You* already boasting sales of more than 25 million, it had something to prove.

Being a past recipient of an Oscar herself, Celine Dion was invited to perform her hit single, 'Because You Loved Me', at the 1997 Academy Awards Ceremony. A series of unexpected events led to her performing twice on the evening of the ceremony.

One of the songs to be showcased at the event was the theme from the Barbra Streisand movie, The Mirror Has Two Faces. It was to have been sung by Natalie Cole, who had to cancel at short notice due to illness. The natural choice to sing it instead was Streisand herself, but she was not certain she would be able to attend the show

and declined. The slot for the song was already scheduled, so the producers of the show asked if Celine Dion would be prepared to appear twice, singing the Streisand song in addition to her own. This was the night before the event itself, but Celine said she would love to perform: 'of course, when you love to sing!'

She had no time to rehearse the song or commit the lyric to memory but was determined not to let the opportunity of singing with a full orchestra before an international audience go to waste. She asked for the words of the song to be taped to her microphone stand.

On the night, as Celine was about to go on stage to perform the Natalie Cole song, she heard that Streisand had made it and was in the audience. Celine recalls that while singing the song she looked out into the vast hall and noticed two striking, green eyes—Streisand's—looking up at her from the front row.

ABOVE: *Celine celebrates with Lionel Ritchie at the World Music Awards in 1997.*

They met after the show, and the next day Celine received a bouquet of flowers from Barbra with a note suggesting that they sing together. René Angelil took the suggestion seriously and contacted Streisand's manager to set things up. Celine was more than thrilled at the prospect. 'She's my favourite singer,' she has said. 'I've been singing along with her.'

Celine drew upon many of her friends and contacts within the music industry to assemble an impressive array of guest talent to sing with her on the album she called 'the album of my life'. The inspirational line-up of collaborators reads like a *Who's Who* of award-winning pop history.

For the track, 'Tell Him', also released as a single, Celine sings with fellow vocal legend, Barbra Streisand. Celine was thrilled finally to be working with Barbra, reporting, 'It was the best experience I've had in show business. Another dream come true. She's a person I've looked up to all my life, as an artist and a woman.'

'Tell Him' was written by the Foster-Thompson team with Walter Afanasieff (who produces much of the album). It was intended to be the first single from *Let's Talk About Love* and, as a promotional stunt, was beamed via satellite to radio stations across the USA on the evening of October 7. Barbra Streisand also included a version of the song on her own album, *Higher Ground*.

The two singers did not meet in the studio to record the track. Barbra laid down her vocal first, and then Celine sang her part, following the lead and expression that Barbra had already established. They were seen singing together on the video, and the two singers did later sing the song together just for their own amusement. 'We sang it together for the pleasure,' explained Celine, 'For the thrill—for my thrill.'

For 'The Reason' Celine Dion teamed up with another of her idols, Carole King, who wrote the track and also provided piano accompaniment. Celine said of working with Carole King, 'I felt like she was my sister.' For this offering the veteran producer Sir George Martin was brought in. This project marked one of the final professional commissions undertaken by Martin prior to his retirement. His five-decade career had brought him to prominence for historic work as the producer of The Beatles. Celine speaks of her association with Martin with great affection, saying that 'Knowing him and working with him is something I will cherish.'

The Bee Gees wrote, and contributed vocals to the song 'Immortality', which was

produced by Walter Afanasieff. Celine had lived with the music of the Bee Gees since her childhood, when her older brothers and sisters played their records, and she admitted that, 'I cannot believe they wrote me a song!'

For the track 'Never, Never, Never', Celine rose to the challenge of crossing musical genres and sharing the microphone with another legendary talent, the opera virtuoso Luciano Pavarotti. For Celine, this was a thrilling ride through a wish-list of dream collaborators. She calls Pavarotti 'the best singer in the world', saying that, 'having the chance to sing beside him was a new world for me.'

'My Heart Will Go On', from the motion picture soundtrack of the huge—in every respect—*Titanic*, was written by James Horner, one of the industry's most accomplished movie score composers. Released as a single, the track became intrinsically linked with the giant publicity machine attached to the film, and the success of each fed back into the other.

When James Horner presented Celine Dion with the song, it immediately struck a chord within her, and she knew it was right for her and she for it. 'He explained the movie so well to me,' recalls Celine. 'I had tears in my eyes. I went to sing the song before I had seen the movie. I felt so strong and emotional that I was ready to go into the studio and sing.'

James Cameron, the director of *Titanic*, did not initially want any songs in the movie, but René Angelil insisted that James Horner record a demo tape of the song with Celine and present it to Cameron. This was done and, one way or another, the song found its way on to the soundtrack of the film, winning an Oscar for it.

Through the successful songs she has contributed to soundtracks, Celine Dion has become associated with movies: *Beauty and the Beast*, *Sleepless in Seattle*, *Up Close and Personal*, and *Titanic*. She is also attracted to the idea of becoming further involved in movies as an actress. She has dabbled, with her part in *Les Fleurs Sur la Neige* and a more recent cameo in the popular CBS sitcom, *The Nanny*. Does she intend to follow in the footsteps of Whitney Houston and Barbra Streisand, combining her singing career with acting? 'Definitely. My next step is to play in a movie. To be a singer, you have to be an actress. I know I'm an

OPPOSITE: *A Gift of Song, US TV special, 1997 with Bryan Adams.*

actress; I know I can do it. I'm ready to work hard, and I do want to do a movie.'

She insists, though, that if she is to act, then it will be as an actress, as opposed to a singer appearing in a film role. She would love to sing in a movie of course, but not in such a way that she is perceived as Celine Dion appearing in a movie—as Celine Dion with a fictional name. She has, for example, expressed a desire to play the lead in a biography of French torch-song diva Edith Piaf. There have also been rumors that French actor Gerard Depardieu has approached her with an offer to appear opposite him in a forthcoming movie and has been negotiating with Angelil.

The album *Let's Talk About Love* was released in several different editions. The Asian edition included a track entitled, 'Be the Man'. This was written as the title song for a major drama series on Japan's Fuji television network, marking the second time that Celine Dion has provided a song, again penned and produced by David Foster, for a Japanese TV series.

Another edition saw Celine extending her linguistic scope with the inclusion of an original song sung in Spanish. This track, 'Amar Haciendo El Amore', appears on

pressings destined for Latin America, Europe, and Canada.

Dion's choice to work with so many huge names was in one way a great risk. The likes of Streisand and Pavarotti hold little appeal for the pop-rock audience loyal to Dion. The inclusion of these guest performers may well bridge genres, but it also ran the risk of alienating the younger audience required to continue the level of sales success Dion had grown used to. Many Top-40-orientated radio stations did not place the duet 'Tell Him' on their play-lists, though it was aired on contemporary stations that target the older listener.

'Tell Him' was intended to be the first single from *Let's Talk About Love*, but Sony canceled its initial release in the USA, even though the CDs had already been pressed. They decided instead to wait a little longer and issue 'My Heart Will Go On' as the debut single. This was a far safer bet, the tie-in with the movie soundtrack for *Titanic* ensuring immediate profile. 'Tell Him' did perform respectably overseas and climbed to number three in the UK charts.

Some influential critics had less than kind things to say about the album on its release. The *Sunday Times* in the UK concluded that, 'If we were rating the album out of 10, the music would probably merit a four, but the string-pulling, favour-calling deal-making and general networking of Dion's management deserves a 10.'

The *New York Times* called the offering, 'plush and bloated', while the *Toronto Sun* referred to 'vocal pyrotechnics without much soul'. Other journalists were calling Dion an 'old fogy before age 30', taking pains to point out the ages of her collaborators: Streisand and King were 55, the Brothers Gibb ranged from 48 to 51, Pavarotti was 62, and Sir George Martin was 71.

Celine Dion countered these critics by saying, 'I don't want to be hip; I'm looking for class. I'm just being myself.' She also points out that, 'I've made enough money for the rest of my life. Every time I have recorded an album, it's with my heart, my soul. All my songs are hits to me. I just worked with the best people in the world. If this album doesn't work, I've still had the time of my life.'

As for accusations of being 'over produced', Celine believes that, 'Being over produced, to me, is not a bad thing; it's a big thing, it's big time, it's Gone With The Wind.'

OPPOSITE: *The queen of song: Celine performs at a Royal Command Performance.*

The huge sales of the album speak for themselves. *Let's Talk About Love* is one of the fastest selling albums, by any artist in world history. Celine has outsold Streisand and could Elvis Presley, with sales exceeding 45 million records in two years. For the first part of 1998 her records were selling faster than those of any preceding recording artist in history.

Although she has claimed not to be a political person, Celine Dion has used her music to try to make a difference. She is the equivalent of a royal emissary for Québec. As such she was invited to sing at the Whitehouse for the inauguration of Bill Clinton, which she described as, 'a thrill'. She explained that she was honored by the invitation: 'When you're not from the United States and they ask you to come and join the family of the United States, the American people, to share a very important moment, it's special, it's a big honor.'

ABOVE: *A lighter moment: Celine appears in TV's Sesame Street.*

OPPOSITE: *Not a 'political person', for Celine emotion and the soul are most important.*

The statement implicit in all of Celine's tenuous associations with political events is that people should consider emotions and the human soul in all aspects of life, and especially in politics, where these dimensions are universally overlooked. Music crosses barriers of language and culture; it can unite and it can inflame.

Whenever she performs, Celine Dion symbolizes the power of the dream. Her success is undeniable testimony that faith in your own talents and perseverance can win through. There is nothing wrong with having your head in the clouds, so long as your feet remain firmly on the ground.

In April 1998 Celine Dion joined an array of stars, including Aretha Franklin, Mariah Carey, Gloria Estefan, and (another Canadian export) Shania Twain, in a concert to campaign for the reintroduction of music education in America's public schools.

As we approach the new millennium, what lies in store for Celine Dion? Having already succeeded so spectacularly, she is still setting new challenges for herself. In

addition to her intention to branch out into acting, she has taken up golf.

Golf is a game she can relate to as a metaphor for her singing career, indeed for life itself. She started playing to be with René, who has been playing for more than 25 years. As with her approach to most ventures, she takes her leisure pursuits seriously, and took a month off for golf lessons. She likens the game to show business, pointing out that you need focus, concentration and control, and that, 'You want to beat your last performance, you are in competition with yourself.'

On a personal level, she and René hope to start a family, though Celine intends to devote herself fully to the task when the opportunity arises. 'My baby will need all my energy. I need to give my baby some time, and right now, I think performer, I think stage, I think tour.'

A recent market survey revealed that Celine Dion is the most famous, recognizable, and revered personality in Québec. A poll conducted by Leger & Leger revealed that more than 90 per cent of people have favorable opinions of Dion, whereas only 68.5 per cent have anything good to say about Premier Lucien Bouchard, who is considered

ABOVE: *More challenges for Celine in the next millennium?*

OPPOSITE: *At the 70th Academy Awards in Los Angeles.*

very popular in political terms. These factors were almost certainly taken into account when Celine was appointed as Canada's spokeswoman for Diet Coke. In the USA Celine Dion has reached a level of fame that has placed her on the cover of *Time Magazine*.

In May 1998, Celine was appointed both to the Order of Canada (one of the most prestigious awards Canada can bestow) and to the National Order of Québec (the highest honor of her home province) in Québec City.

Looking back over her illustrious career, does Celine have any regrets? Apparently not, for Celine declares, 'I really appreciate each thing that I've accomplished, and I've enjoyed it completely. I don't want to look behind me. I expect a lot from myself in the future. I always hoped and wished that everything was going to be very beautiful in life, and especially in show business, and it's exactly the way I thought.'

ABOVE: *A chic Celine in Paris for Chanel's winter 97–98 winter show.*

OPPOSITE: *And an elegant guest at Dior's showing for winter 98–99.*

SINGLES

Ce N'était Qu'un Reve (1981)
L'amour Viendra (1981)
La Voix du Bon Dieu (1981)
D'Amour ou D'Amitié (1983)
Un Amour Pour Moi (1984)
Une Colombe (1984)
Mon Rêve de Toujours (1984)
C'est Pour Toi (1985)
C'est Pour Vivre (1985)
Fais Ce Que Tu Voudras (1985)
Délivre-moi (1987)
Incognito (1987)
Lolita (1987)
On Traverse un Miroir (1987)
Comme un Coeur Froid (1988)
D'abords C'est Quoi L'amour (1988)
(If There Was) Any Other Way (1990)
Where Does My Heart Beat Now (1990)
Last To Know (1991)

(You Make Me Feel Like a) Natural Woman (1995)
Because You Loved Me (1996)
It's All Coming Back To me Now (1996)
All By Myself (1997)
To Love You More (1997)
Tell Him (1997 with Barbara Streisend)
My Heart Will Go On (1997)

ALBUMS

La Voix du Bon Dieu (1981)
Celine Chante Noel (1981)
Tellemente J'ai D'amour (1982)
Chantes et Contes de Noel (1983)
Les Chemins de Ma Maison (1983)
Les Plus Grands Succès de Celine Dion (1984)
Melanie (1984)
Les Oiseaux du Bonheur (1984 compilation released in Europe only)

Discography

Ziggy (1991)
Have A Heart (1991)
Beauty And The Beast (1991 with Peabo Bryson)
If You Asked Me To (1992)
Des Mots Qui Sonnent (1992)
Je Danse Dans Ma Tête (1992)
Nothing Broken But My Heart (1992)
Love Can Move Mountains (1992)
Water From The Moon (1993)
When I Fall in Love (1993 with Clive Griffin)
Did You Give Enough Love? (1993)
The Power of Love (1993)
Misled (1994)
Think Twice (1994)
L'amour Existe Encore (1994)
Only One Road (1994)
Pour Que Tu M'aimes Encore (1995)
Je Suis Pas (1995)

Celine Dion en Concert (1985 live)
C'est Pour Toi (1985)
Le Chansons en Or (1986 compilation)
Incognito (1987)
Vivre (1989 compilation, released in Europe only)
Unison (1990)
Dion Chante Plamondon (1991 aka Des Mots Qui Sonnet)
Celine Dion (1992)
The Colour of My Love (1993)
Les Première Années (1993 compilation)
Celine Dion à L'Olympia (1994 live)
D'eux (1995 aka The French Album)
Falling Into You (1996)
Falling Into You (1996 Australian edition with bonus live CD)
Celine Dion: The Collection (1996 promotional compilation, not released commercially)

Gold Volume 1 (1996 compilation, released in Canada only)
Gold Volume 2 (1996 compilation, released in Canada only)
Live à Paris (1996 live, released in Canada only)
Let's Talk About Love (1997)

GUEST VOCAL APPEARANCES AND DUETS

True Love (1989 album by Dan Hill)
TRACK: Wishful Thinking (duet with Dan Hill)

Spellbound (1989 album by Billy Newton Davis)
TRACK: Can't Live With You, Can't Live Without You (duet with Billy Newton Davis)

Listen To Me (1989 single)
duet with Warren Wiebe

Tycoon (1992 compilation soundtrack album)
TRACKS: Ziggy (English version) and Tonight We Dance - Extravagance

Beauty And The Beast (1992 soundtrack album)
TRACK: Beauty And The Beast (duet with Peabo Bryson)

Sleepless in Seattle (1993 soundtrack album)
TRACK: When I Fall in Love (duet with Clive Griffin)

Mario Pelchat (1993 album by Mario Pelchat)
TRACK: Plus Haut Que Moi (duet with Mario Pelchat)

Cosmopolitan Vol #7 (1993 compilation album)
TRACK: If There Were Any Other Way

Christmas Album (1993)
TRACK: The Christmas Song

Kubaya (1994 compilation album)

TRACK: Send Me a Lover

In Between Dances (1995 compilation album for the Canadian Breast Cancer Research Initiative)
TRACK: Send Me a Lover

Tapestry Revisted (1995 tribute album to Carole King)
TRACK: (You Make Me Feel Like a) Natural Woman

Grammy Award Nominees (1995 compilation album)
TRACK: The Power of Love

Women for Women 2 (1996 compilation album)
TRACK: Send Me a Lover

Siren Song: A Celebration of Women in Music (1996 compilation album)
TRACK: If You Asked Me To

Amigos (1996 album by Paul Anka)
TRACK: Mejor Decir Adios (duet with Paul Anka)

For Our Children Too (1996 compilation album to benefit Pediatric AIDS Foundation)
TRACKS: Brahms Lullaby and Love Lights the World (with David Foster, Peabo Bryson and Color Me Badd)

Grammy Award Nominees (1997 compilation album)
TRACK: Because You Loved Me

Greatest Dance Album in the World (1997 compilation album)
TRACK: It's All Coming Back to Me Now

Diana Princess of Wales (1997 tribute compilation album)
TRACK: Because You Loved Me

Superstar Christmas (1997 compilation album)
The Christmas Song

Index